Living Life
Over 50

Secrets to Finding Love, Your Vibrant Style & What's Next For You

Dr. Geneva J. Williams

DEDICATION

To all women over 50—you make life worth living.

This book is dedicated to my mom, Blanche Hillen Jones, whose love and wisdom shaped me into the vibrant, impactful woman I am today. To my family and friends—thank you for your unwavering support.

Contents

Lifelong Friendship, New Chapters

Some friendships are seasonal; others last a lifetime. But then, there are the rare, extraordinary ones—friendships that shape who you are, push you to become your best self and walk with you through every chapter of life.

My friendship with Geneva is one of those. For more than fifty-five years, we have been side by side, navigating life's transitions, celebrating victories, and holding each other up during the toughest moments. She is more than my best friend; she is my sister. I am the godmother to her children and a witness to every joy and every heartbreak of her life.

And she has been the same for me.

As an award-winning educator and principal of Thurgood Marshall Academy for Learning and Social Change in Harlem, I've dedicated my life to transforming young lives and building strong communities. But my journey in education began just like Geneva's—at Morgan State University, where we pledged Alpha Kappa Alpha Sorority together, unaware that we were forging a bond that would last a lifetime.

From my years leading the transformation of Thurgood Marshall Academy into an International Baccalaureate world school to helping rebuild the Central Harlem community to my current role as director of the Harlem Renaissance Educational Pipeline, I have never believed in slowing down, only in expanding. Just as Geneva has continuously evolved—leading, mentoring, and embracing new opportunities—I, too, have embraced new chapters in service to our community.

Through every transition, we have shown each other what's possible—what it means to step into the unknown with courage and to trust that reinvention is not about age but about vision. When Geneva made the life-changing decision to move to Detroit, leaving the East Coast she had always called home, I encouraged her, reminding her that reinvention is not about where you are but about who you are becoming.

When I transitioned from leading Thurgood Marshall Academy to directing the Harlem Renaissance Educational Pipeline, she celebrated my refusal to accept retirement as an endpoint but rather as a launching pad for new impact.

I watched with pride as Geneva reinvented herself as an author and public speaker, launching a successful podcast and becoming a sought-after voice for leaders over 50. Meanwhile, I continued to expand my own vision of what's possible, taking our successful educational model to create a broader impact throughout the country.

We've both embraced the principle that life after 50 isn't about slowing down—it's about stepping up into new forms of leadership and service.

Our friendship exemplifies what I've seen Geneva champion throughout this book—the power of supportive relationships, especially after 50. In a world that often dismisses people of our generation, having someone who truly sees your potential, celebrates your victories, and holds you up during challenges isn't just meaningful—it's essential for thriving in these vibrant years.

When Geneva told me she was writing this book, I knew it was time. Time for her to put into words what I have watched her live. Time for her to share the wisdom, the strategies, and the deeply personal lessons that have shaped her journey.

Because this book isn't about her—it's about you, the reader. It's about what's next. It's about claiming your power and designing the life you want, no matter where you are on the journey.

This book couldn't be more timely. As we navigate an ever-changing world after 50, Geneva's insights are more relevant than ever. While she speaks primarily to women's experiences, her core messages about reinvention and purposeful living resonate with anyone seeking to make their **later years their greater years.**

So, as you turn these pages, know that Geneva writes this from a place of love, experience, and an unwavering belief that your best chapter is still ahead. I have had the honor of witnessing her journey firsthand.

As Geneva has done for thousands of women, she, too, has done for me and my family—by living as an example of what's possible. Watching her navigate transitions with purpose and conviction has been a reminder that the next chapter is always ours to create.

And I know one thing for sure: if you are ready to step into your next season with purpose, confidence, and joy—there is no better guide than Geneva Williams.

Dr. Sandye P. Johnson,
Director, Harlem Renaissance Educational Pipeline, and Chair, Abyssinian Development Corporation

Principal, Thurgood Marshall Academy for Learning and Social Change

Time Warner Principal of Excellence national awardee

Black Women's Agenda "Inspirational Educator" awardee

Foreword

By Jacqueline T. Hill

Beverly paused for a minute and looked around the room. The smiles, claps, and cheers from family and friends, each face bringing back a memory of past times.

The fifty-five candles, now all blown, sent spiraling, wisps of smoke into the atmosphere as the cheers gave way to stillness and the expected speech.

Beverly smiled, looked down at her notes and started to read the words that she'd prepared earlier. The usual words thanking her family for coming, how life was exciting and she was looking forward to the next fifty years but in truth, she didn't feel it.

She felt lost. As if her life no longer held purpose or meaning.

She'd always thought that at fifty-five, she'd understand life, would feel fulfilled but instead, she felt overwhelmed and lost. This wasn't what she expected from a life of over 50 years.

I begin this foreword with an anecdote because while standing at the scene of this gathering, I've witnessed Beverly's sense of feeling empty and uncertain. Everyone felt a shift in the atmosphere due to her feelings of displacement. Being in the midst of other women over 50, everyone including I would understand her feelings without spoken words. Above everything during this moment, Beverly desired happiness.

Perhaps you feel like Beverly at different moments in your life. If you are feeling this way, firstly, please know it's normal. One of my favorite books discusses how feeling an inner struggle and despair are common emotions during the mid-fifties.

A sense of it being too late to change things, empty nest syndrome, and the resulting thoughts of 'Who am I? Who do I want to be now?' can create feelings of anxiety and turmoil. But it's never too late to restart a path you loved or to create a new life. Being over 50 is wonderful, and this book is going to take you on a journey to finding love, your vibrant style, and help you with the next steps. In other words, Dr. Geneva will lead you towards a happy life.

As the saying goes, "Happiness is freedom." And, while some women will agree that these words are true, the question now is what does it take to be happy? Does money really buy happiness, or even love? These and many questions linger around being happy in life. Many cling happiness to their achievements and then look for it in the wrong ways and places. The true quest for happiness is knowing fully how efficiently you can put things in order as a priority and pursue the ones that matter. This will make the much-needed difference that your life needs.

Happiness is indeed all we need to scale through the hurdles of life. To breathe the air of freedom and resist the stabbing punches life throws at us every now and then and being extremely happy becomes one of the most effective ways to pick up our broken pieces and keep soldiering against all odds. Some of the mistakes we make in pursuit of happiness are attaching our source of happiness to others or even achievements. Those are some of the wrong ways to go in search of genuine and long-lasting joy. You need to breathe fresh air and not get suffocated at all in a bid to be happy. Happiness isn't bought nor earned; it is a free gift and a must-have for everyone. It rejuvenates the mind and rids it of every form of pessimism, hate, and negativity.

In the race for happiness, it is always good to simplify the pursuit. Use your time and pursue the little things that make the much-needed difference and the people and things that mean the most to you.

This book helps you find happiness and a vibrant life through realistic encounters that will not exhaust you or your resources. Thus, during Dr. Geneva's exploration, she explores three key areas in depth: Finding Love, Your Vibrant Style, and What's Next, and brings them all together into a wonderful, personalized, exciting, happy, vibrant life vision with workable strategies in her *What's Next Framework*. Here's to a wonderful, new, vibrant life—time to read her words!

Why I Wrote This Book

Mary McLeod Bethune said, "Next to God we are indebted to women, first for life itself, and then for making it worth living."

I owe you, my beautiful friends over 50. I want to share and talk about our common experiences and struggles and how being in midlife is phenomenal. Moreover, I want to show you how to get to your "what's next." This is my "debt" to you, showing you how to live a vibrant and impactful life over 50.

Life at this age is a mix of fresh opportunities and unexpected challenges. It's a season of ups and downs, but also one of incredible possibilities. There are great moments that help us become better from hurtful events, however. I want to make sure that you understand how to get through these mixtures.

I liken these bittersweet days to Beauty and the Beast. I can relate to becoming a grandmother and finding gray hairs. My body weight going through changes as well as the relationship with my husband of forty years. My children became independent—moving on with their lives. These ups and downs can feel overwhelming at times.

Often women say to me, "I want to be like you when I grow up." These complimentary words are spoken from women I meet at conferences, whom I meet for the first time when I walk into a room, the gym, church functions, and speaking events. They text me their truest feelings of admiration all of the time. I know that we connect because they see me at this age looking good. Feeling good. Still doing good. Still active.

I make it a priority to respond to them. My life's work has always been about inspiring and creating positive individual and community change, and now my focus is on YOU through this book.

You want to learn how to live the life you want and deserve with style, love, financial freedom, and happiness. That is why I'm sharing these secrets to a vibrant, impactful life with you. As each birthday came to gently nudge me to 55... 60..., I tried to figure out what's next and used a lot of reflective thinking, basically trying to problem-solve.

And what I learned is that having a structured approach— something simple but powerful—can make all the difference. That's why I now use The NEXT Steps Framework to guide women just like you through this journey. So, if you're wondering how to take everything in this book and turn it into real action, be sure to read through to the end, where I share a simple yet powerful way to plan your next step.

I also found myself looking for role models. Understanding the importance of role models burns in my soul, especially for women living the midlife experience.

For many of us, our moms were our role models, coaches, and mentors. As I look at my life in retrospect, I've put together a phenomenal career over the years like my mom. Life has given me the opportunities to teach and be an educator, be active in my community, break records for companies, be a wife to an incredible husband, raise a family, and receive praises for everything like the Proverbs 31 woman.

I'm mirroring my mom. I'm grateful to her for so much, especially for showing me what it takes to "live the life you design," as she used to say to me all the time. After giving a lifetime of herself to her husband, children, students, and community, she continued to make an impact well into her 70s. She instilled in me courage, strength, and the ability to keep it going in life. When I look for role models, she's my first find.

Writing this book allows me to do some role modeling and share a little guidance since I've been there, done that, and am living an amazing life. The advice I give here can help answer your questions about what's next, how to plan it and figure out your upcoming steps.

Seeing a role model is key to navigating what's next. That's why so many women tell me, "I want to be like you when I grow up." Sometimes you need a visual to move along your vision to the next level of your purpose.

And I want to step up to the plate. I'm dedicating myself to making an impact in the lives of women, mentoring, and being a role model. I'm focused on creating platforms for more women to step forward as role models. A platform that's put together in terms of podcasting, starting a new business, being an entrepreneur, speaker, and life coach—allowing me to create space to find and shine the spotlight on more role models.

After changing careers, I recently received recognition as one of the top businesswomen in Michigan. This career change includes writing books, being a public figure at age 70 into fashion, makeup, style, and love. I'm also featured in a nationally televised TV commercial. And, I won a beauty pageant!

I love the women who want to get to their what's next. Hence, I wrote this book to influence your life, to teach you how to make an impact personally, professionally, and in your community.

And I hope to be that role model who shows you how to tap into your creative self to find love, your vibrant style, and what's next.

This book is my way of showing you that your best years aren't behind you—they're right in front of you.

Dr. Geneva

You will always attract what you believe you're worth.

-Unknown

Secret #1

Happiness & Balanced Living

---❋---

I have had countless heart-to-heart conversations with women—some just starting their journey, others well into midlife—about what happiness really means.

Through these conversations, I've learned something powerful: every woman wants joy, purpose, and balance.

Some are healing from past relationships or loss.

Some dream of starting businesses or advancing their careers.

Some are simply trying to figure out what's next.

Many feel out of balance—struggling with weight, sleep, life transitions, or career changes over 50.

Maybe you feel the same way.

Or maybe you can't quite put your finger on what's missing, but you know you want more.

So what's keeping you from feeling truly happy and balanced?

Happiness Begins with Balance

Living a happy, vibrant life isn't just about chasing moments of joy—it's about creating a foundation of balance.

But let's be real.

Many women are caught up in the daily hustle.

- Stress piles up.
- Toxic people linger.
- "Me time" feels impossible to find.

With all that noise, how can you get back to YOU?

How can you find time to breathe, to think, to reconnect with what you really want?

The Power of Mindfulness & Balance

Balance isn't about juggling everything perfectly.

It's about centering yourself so you don't feel like life is spinning out of control.

It's about being intentional with your time, your energy, and your relationships.

When you create balance, you move from just surviving to truly thriving.

- You become fully present. You start cherishing the moment instead of rushing through life.

- You prioritize what matters. Time isn't wasted on things—or people—that drain you.

- You reclaim your happiness. Because happiness isn't something you chase—it's something you build.

How to Feel Good, Look Good & Do Good

When you feel good, look good, and do good, your entire life shifts.

1. Feel Good

- When you feel good, you know who you are.

- You feel confident, clear, and aligned with what truly matters to you.

2. Look Good

- Looking good isn't about vanity—it's about showing up as your best self.

- When you dress in a way that makes you feel vibrant and confident, that energy shines through.

- You own the room. You inspire others. You move through life with power and presence.

3. Do Good

- When you feel good and look good, you have the energy to do good.

- You give back. You create positive influence. You show up for your family, your work, and your community in a way that makes an impact.

You Deserve to Thrive

Happiness and balance don't happen by accident.

They start with you.

They start with small, intentional choices—how you spend your time, how you take care of yourself, and what you allow into your life.

So ask yourself:

What's one thing you can do today to bring more balance into your life?

Because when you create balance, you create the space for happiness to grow.

You can rise up from anything.

You can completely recreate yourself.

Nothing is permanent.

You're not stuck.

You have choices.

You can think new thoughts.

You can learn something new.

You can create new habits.

All that matters is that you decide

today and never look back.

-Unknown

Secret #2

Moving Towards Self-Love

———✷———

Self-love is talked about everywhere—but do we truly understand it?

For some, self-love means setting boundaries and saying no without guilt. For others, it's about prioritizing health, rest, and emotional well-being. No two people love themselves in the same way.

But here's what I know for sure:

Self-love fuels a vibrant life.

When stress piles up, when you feel stuck, when your body is drained, self-love is what lifts you back up.

If you're feeling burdened, overwhelmed, or like you're in a dark hole you can't climb out of, self-love is what pulls you forward.

Self-Love is a Lifeline

I know this because I've lived it.

A few years ago, I experienced unimaginable loss. I lost my husband and both of my parents within a short period of time.

I had to write three obituaries. I had to take on responsibilities I never expected.

I was drowning in grief.

And even though I had spent years teaching others how to rise through challenges, I found myself struggling to do the same.

It would have been easy to stay stuck in that place of sorrow. But I knew I had a choice:

I could either let grief consume me or use my power within to pull myself out.

I chose self-love.

And I learned something:

Self-love isn't just a feeling. It's an action.

It's about making daily choices that prioritize your well-being, your peace, and your joy.

Vibrant Living is Daily Reinvention

Self-love isn't a quick fix. It's a journey.

It's about turning pain into growth.

It's about becoming wiser and sharper with age.

It's about waking up every day and deciding:

"I am creating my life exactly as I want it."

Now, that's a powerful place to be.

Steps to Embrace Self-Love & Vibrant Living

1. Buy yourself something special. A new outfit, a piece of jewelry—something that reminds you that you are worth investing in.

2. Write down the biggest challenge you want to overcome. Putting it on paper makes it real—and makes it something you can tackle.

3. Put your phone aside for an hour and do something just for you. No notifications. No distractions. Just time for yourself.

4. Detox your social media. Remove anyone who doesn't bring joy, inspiration, or positivity into your life.

5. Have quiet time for prayer or reflection. Your soul needs stillness just as much as your body needs rest.

6. Read the book you never have time for. Let yourself get lost in a new world, a new idea, or a new perspective.

7. Laugh—loud, deep, and often. Laughter is one of the best ways to lift your spirit instantly.

8. Move your body. Whether it's yoga, a walk, or dancing in your living room, movement is self-care.

9. Put on your favorite outfit. Do your makeup, spritz your favorite perfume, and go somewhere special.

Self-Love is the Foundation for Everything

When you feel good, you make yourself a priority.

When you look good, you radiate confidence.

When you do good, you spread that energy to the world around you.

Self-love isn't selfish. It's the foundation for a vibrant life.

So start today.

Choose yourself.

Because when you do, everything else begins to fall into place

The comeback is always stronger than the setback.

-Unknown

Secret #3

Rebuild Your Life

———✦———

Time brings change—and with it, incredible opportunities. Who knew retirement could open the door to such amazing experiences? Vibrant living feels incredible—these are my best days yet. Every experience—good or bad—prepares you for something greater. The key to growing and becoming is allowing yourself to just be and fulfill all of the dreams and desires you've held on to for years.

Since retiring, I've stepped into new entrepreneurial and leadership roles that continue to shape my story. As my journey unfolds, I'm helping other women do the same. I show you how to rebuild your life at this moment. I love walking with you and guiding you to a place of reinventing yourself to become a creative self. In fact, I've discovered a few rules that'll transition you now. Continue to read on.

Here are 14 ways to rebuild your life—starting now. Being over 50 doesn't mean life slows down. If anything, it's the perfect time for a new beginning. Reinvention begins anytime you're ready. Your 20's, 30s, and 40's are in the past. You've lived through incredible moments—but the best is still ahead.

1. Use creativity in your home life. That kitchen or living room remodel you once dreamed of? Why not do it now? Get creative, plan it out, and bring your vision to life.

2. Plan to live in the moment. Stop waiting for the "perfect time." Life is happening now—enjoy it fully.

3. Redesign your space—and your life. Many of my friends have refreshed their homes and their mindsets. We hold each other accountable.

4. Give back to your community. Volunteer, mentor, or simply be present. Helping others is one of the best ways to rebuild yourself.

5. Do what you love now and in the future. You've spent years doing what needed to be done. Now, it's time to do what you love.

6. Stay in your happy place. Surround yourself with people, activities, and environments that bring you joy. Happiness is a choice—protect it.

7. Secure your financial future. Plan for your financial stability. Save, invest wisely, and make sure you have what you need—not just for today, but for years to come.

8. Increase the value of what you own. Whether it's your home, skills, or experiences, invest in things that appreciate over time.

9. Embrace technology. Don't fear it—ask your grandkids, take a class, or just start experimenting. The digital world isn't just for the young.

10. Think long-term, not short-term. You still have decades ahead—make decisions with the long game in mind.

11. Move your body every day. Walk, dance, stretch—whatever keeps you active and feeling good.

12. Nourish yourself with good food. A healthy diet fuels a vibrant life.

13. Stay connected. Reconnect with old friends, make new ones, and nurture relationships that matter.

14. Keep learning. Never stop growing. Read, take classes, or explore new skills to keep your mind sharp.

There is no force more powerful

than a woman determined to rise.

- Dorothy Dandridge

Secret #4

Breaking Forth To Live Vibrantly

The golden jubilee—a milestone, a turning point, a moment to celebrate how far you've come and to embrace what's next. Fifty years of life. Half a century of experiences, lessons, challenges, and triumphs. Now, it's time to prepare for the next chapter, one where you don't just exist—you thrive.

Many emotions surface in midlife—happiness, fulfillment, and gratitude, but also fear, uncertainty, and confusion. You've spent years building a career, raising a family, and taking care of everyone else. Now, for the first time, you may find yourself wondering: What about me?

For as long as you can remember, leadership has come naturally to you. You've taken care of people, managed responsibilities, and inspired those around you. But this new chapter may feel unfamiliar. You may worry that your best years are behind you. You may wonder if you still have the same drive, energy, or purpose. But here's the truth—you are not done yet.

Embracing Change Without Fear

The most constant thing in life is change. And yet, change is what makes so many people feel stuck. It's easy to stay in what's familiar, even if it no longer excites you. But midlife isn't an ending—it's a fresh start.

You can still live a happy, vibrant, and deeply fulfilled life, no matter what transitions you're facing. The key? Stepping boldly into the unknown with intention, purpose, and a willingness to redefine success on your own terms.

No one has life completely figured out. And the good news is—you don't have to. What you do need is a personalized life plan that helps you navigate this transition, one that is built on your passions, strengths, and deepest desires.

Think of it as an action plan for your best years yet—one that gives you clarity, direction, and a renewed sense of purpose.

Designing Your Personalized Life Plan

A company wouldn't operate without a strategy. Why should your life be any different? A personal life plan isn't about rigid goals or overwhelming to-do lists. It's a guide that helps you stay focused, motivated, and intentional about your future.

Here's what your plan should include:

1. A Clear Vision: Where do you see yourself in the next five years? What excites you? What do you want more of in your life?

2. Meaningful Goals: Identify what truly matters to you—whether it's travel, entrepreneurship, health, or deepening relationships.

3. Steps to Take: Break your goals into actionable steps. What can you do today to move closer to your vision?

4. Resources & Support: Who and what can help you succeed? Build a network of people who inspire, support, and encourage you.

5. A Commitment to Growth: Life is about learning, evolving, and expanding. Stay open to new experiences, knowledge, and opportunities.

The Power of Reinvention

Aging isn't about slowing down. It's about elevating. Every woman who has successfully reinvented herself started by making one decision—to no longer settle for a life that didn't excite her.

Take a look at inspiring women around you. Many have launched businesses, stepped into leadership roles, found love again, or completely changed careers in their 50s, 60s, and beyond. The one thing they all have in common? They decided they were just getting started.

Your next chapter is waiting, but you have to take the first step.

Your Personalized Blueprint for a Vibrant Life

1. Think Big, Act Boldly: Let go of small thinking. What if nothing was holding you back? What would you do next?

2. Embrace Growth Over Comfort: If it doesn't challenge you, it won't change you. Get comfortable with being a beginner again.

3. Take Daily Action: Small, consistent steps create major transformations. One decision today can change everything.

4. Surround Yourself with the Right People: Seek out friendships and mentors who elevate you, inspire you, and hold you accountable.

5. Give Yourself Permission to Dream Again: Your goals don't expire. If you're still here, you still have purpose.

It's Your Time. Own it.

This is not the time to fade into the background or shrink yourself. This is the time to step fully into your power, wisdom, and experience.

You've spent years taking care of others, showing up, and doing what was expected of you. Now, it's time to pour that same energy into yourself.

The best years of your life aren't behind you—they are in front of you. The only question is: What will you do with them?

You don't make progress by standing on the
sidelines whimpering and complaining. You make
progress by implementing ideas.

-Shirley Chisholm

Secret #5

Breaking Forth As A Power Sensation

————— ❖ —————

I begin with a quote:

"You have to reinvent the self to become a creative (vibrant) self." — bell hooks

To live a vibrant life, you have to reclaim your power and redefine what's possible.

Women over 50 are taking back their lives, stepping into new identities, and embracing fearless reinvention. These women are power sensations—not because they never faced challenges, but because they refused to let those challenges define them.

The younger women are strong. But the seasoned women? They know the way.

They've walked through storms and come out wiser. They've faced hardships and learned how to rise. They are the matriarchs, the leaders, the quiet forces reshaping the world—often without recognition, but always with impact.

The Power of Women Over 50

Women today are more alive than ever because they've faced life's challenges head-on. They've reinvented themselves, started businesses, taken on leadership roles, and redefined success on their own terms.

They lead with resilience. They show faith in the face of adversity. They give wisdom to the next generation. They take on new challenges with a boldness that only comes with experience.

There's something unstoppable about a woman who has lived, learned, and decided that she is not finished yet.

The Fearless Women Leading the Way

Let's look at powerful women over 50 who are leading by example:

- Maxine Waters (80 years old) serves as a U.S. Representative. Before politics, she was a garment factory worker and a telephone operator. Now, she's an unapologetic leader, still making waves.

- Nancy Pelosi (78 years old) grew up in a political household, became a mother of five, and later became the 52nd Speaker of the U.S. House of Representatives.

- Janice Bryant Howroyd (69 years old) is the first African American woman to run a billion-dollar business. She grew up in the segregated South and launched her company with just $1,000.

- Susan Zirinsky (66 years old) has been with CBS News since 1972. In her 60s, she shattered barriers by becoming the first female president of CBS News.

These women weren't handed their success. They built it.

And so can you.

What It Means to Be a Power Sensation

Being a power sensation isn't about fame or status—it's about how you carry yourself, how you show up, and how you own your space.

Women over 50 are:

- **Trailblazers**—not afraid to challenge outdated norms.

- **Visionaries**—embracing new dreams at any age.

- **Leaders**—mentoring, inspiring, and paving the way.

Many of these women have faced being overlooked. Some were pushed out of jobs or ignored in boardrooms. Others saw opportunities vanish because of their age.

But instead of fading away, they built their own doors to walk through.

They launched businesses. They ran for office. They embraced entrepreneurship. They found new passions. They refused to be silenced.

That's what it means to break forth as a power sensation.

How to Step Into Your Power

1. Own Your Story. Your experiences—every triumph and every setback—have shaped you. They are your superpower.

2. Speak with Authority. You've lived. You've learned. You don't need permission to take up space.

3. Stay Visible. Don't shrink yourself. Show up boldly in your personal life, career, or community.

4. Build a Legacy. Make an impact, whether it's mentoring young women, starting a new venture, or simply living unapologetically.

5. Refuse to Be Defined by Age. Age doesn't limit you—mindset does. Break free from the belief that your best years are behind you.

You Are Just Getting Started

Women over 50 are leading, creating, and thriving. They are proving that age is an asset, not a setback.

And now, it's your turn.

You have the wisdom, the experience, and the fire to create something incredible.

The world needs your voice, your leadership, and your presence.

You are a power sensation. Step into it.

Find people who will make you better.

-Michelle Obama

Secret #6

Be Happy

Happiness is not age-bound. It is a choice.

You can be happy at 50 and beyond if that is what you want. Being happy means you are joyous or content with all you've achieved over the years. Too often, people believe that as they get older, their best moments of joy and fulfillment are behind them. But the truth is, **you can be happier than ever—right now, at this stage of life.**

Happiness isn't about waiting for the perfect conditions. It's about making a **deliberate choice** to find joy, embrace gratitude, and live fully **every single day.**

The Power of Choosing Happiness

Science backs this up: happiness has profound effects on your mental, emotional, and physical health. Studies show that happy people live longer, have stronger immune systems, and maintain better heart health.

But beyond science, you already know this to be true. Think about a time when you felt genuinely happy— maybe it was a simple moment, laughing with a close friend, feeling the sun on your skin, or waking up with excitement for the day ahead. Happiness changes everything.

And yet, many people spend their lives chasing it, believing it's something they'll find later—after they get the job, the house, the relationship, the money.

But happiness doesn't wait. It's something you cultivate right now, in this moment.

The Myths About Happiness

Let's clear up a few things:

- Happiness isn't about being happy all the time. No one is. Life brings struggles, losses, and challenges—but happiness is about how you navigate them.

- Happiness isn't tied to money. While financial stability is important, studies show that after a certain level of comfort, more money doesn't equal more joy.

- Happiness isn't found in external achievements. Promotions, awards, or recognition feel good, but true happiness comes from within.

So, if happiness isn't about waiting for the perfect life, then what is it about?

How to Cultivate Happiness Every Day

1. Shift Your Mindset.

Happiness begins with perspective. If you constantly focus on what's missing, you'll never feel like you have enough. Instead, train your mind to see what's already good in your life.

2.   Practice Gratitude.

Take a moment every day to acknowledge three things you're grateful for. It could be big or small—a phone call from a loved one, the ability to move your body, or a warm cup of coffee. Gratitude rewires your brain for joy.

3.   Surround Yourself with Joyful People.

Energy is contagious. If you're around negativity all the time, it will drain you. But when you spend time with people who uplift, inspire, and make you laugh, your happiness grows.

4.   Let Go of the Past.

Carrying past regrets, anger, or resentment steals your peace. You can't change the past, but you can change how you move forward. Choose to release what no longer serves you.

5.   Engage in Activities That Light You Up.

What makes you feel alive? Is it dancing, painting, traveling, or simply spending time in nature? Do more of what makes you happy—and do it often.

6.   Take Care of Your Body.

Happiness and health are connected. Move your body, eat nourishing food, and get enough rest. You'll be amazed at how much better you feel when you prioritize your well-being.

7. Stop Seeking Validation from Others.

You don't need anyone's permission to be happy. Your happiness is yours to define. Live in a way that feels good to you—regardless of what others think.

8. Laugh More.

Laughter truly is medicine. Find reasons to laugh every day—whether it's watching something funny, sharing stories with friends, or just learning to laugh at yourself.

Happiness is an Inside Job

No one else is responsible for your happiness. Not your partner. Not your job. Not your children.

You have the power to cultivate joy, independent of your circumstances.

Happiness is in the small moments—a quiet morning, a heartfelt conversation, a favorite song playing in the car. It's always there, waiting for you to claim it.

Your Best, Happiest Years Are Ahead

Forget the myth that happiness fades with age. In reality, it deepens.

Why? Because by this stage in life, you know yourself better. You're more confident, more self-aware, and less willing to waste time on things that don't matter.

The best years of your life aren't behind you. They're ahead.

And happiness? It's not a distant goal—it's a daily practice.

So start today. Be happy. Not tomorrow. Not next week. Now.

Never underestimate the impact that

you may have on someone else's life.

--Izzy Be

Secret #7

Fashion Matters

I have always loved fashion.

It's not just about clothes—it's about self-expression, confidence, and feeling good in your own skin.2

But as I got older, I noticed something. Society seemed to have an unspoken rule that once a woman hit 50, she had to start dressing a certain way—toning it down, playing it safe, becoming "age-appropriate."

I never subscribed to that.

I believe that fashion is about authenticity, not age. You should dress in a way that makes you feel good and look good—on your terms.

Breaking the Myth: Style Has No Age Limit

For years, women over 50 have been told to dress "appropriately"—as if turning a certain age means you have to trade in your personal style for something dull and outdated.

But here's the truth: Your sense of style should grow with you, not disappear.

- If you love bold colors—wear them.

- If you feel powerful in heels—rock them.

- If you adore statement accessories—own them.

The key is dressing in a way that celebrates who you are now, not who society expects you to be.

How to Own Your Style Over 50

1. Dress for Yourself, Not Others.

Your style should be a reflection of who you are—not what someone else thinks is "appropriate." Wear what makes you feel confident and beautiful.

2. Invest in Pieces That Make You Feel Powerful.

A great blazer, a well-fitted dress, or a pair of fabulous shoes can do wonders for your confidence.

3. Choose Colors That Energize You.

Gone are the days of playing it safe with neutrals. If you love bright colors, wear them. Your wardrobe should reflect your personality.

4. Don't Be Afraid to Mix Classic with Trendy.

Style isn't about choosing between "young" or "old" looks. It's about finding a balance between timeless pieces and modern touches that make you feel fresh and fabulous.

5. Tailoring is Your Best Friend.

Clothes should fit your body—not the other way around. The right fit can elevate any outfit, making you look and feel amazing.

6. Accessories Make the Difference.

A bold necklace, a great handbag, or a stylish pair of sunglasses can take your look to the next level.

7. Shoes Matter—Choose Comfort and Style.

You don't have to give up heels if you love them. But you can also find stylish flats, wedges, and sneakers that keep you looking chic while staying comfortable.

8. Confidence is the Best Outfit.

You can wear the most beautiful outfit in the world, but if you don't own it with confidence, it won't shine.

Style is a Statement—At Any Age

I've never believed in "dressing my age."

I dress for who I am, how I feel, and how I want to show up in the world.

And if you love fashion like I do, don't let age take that away from you.

Fashion is a form of self-care, self-expression, and self-confidence. It's a way to tell the world, "I am still here, I am still vibrant, and I am still me."

So wear what makes you feel beautiful, powerful, and alive.

Because style doesn't fade with age—it evolves.

Success is self-care mastery.

-Karen Taylor Bass

Secret #8

Find Love *Again*

—— ❈ ——

Love doesn't come with an expiration date.

It doesn't matter if you're 30, 50, or 75—**love is always possible.**

I know this because I lived it.

My Love Story: When You Know, You Know

I was in my 20s when I experienced **love at first sight.**

At the time, I thought I already had love figured out. There was someone I had been seeing, a man I thought I was crazy about. That week, I had planned to visit him, convinced that he might be "the one."

But then my mother asked me to do something that changed everything.

She was leading a national conference in Detroit and wanted me to come and speak. I agreed—reluctantly. I had other plans. But when your mother asks, you do it.

So I went to Detroit. And that's where I met **him.**

A tall, dark, handsome man. The kind of man you don't just see—you **feel.**

It was a **Wednesday** when we met.

By **Friday,** we were shopping for furniture.

Because we knew. **We knew we were going to get married.**

Ten months later, we were.

And for the next **40 years,** we built a life together—a love so strong that even when cancer took him, it didn't take the love. That love still lives in me today.

Would we still be married today if he were here? Absolutely.

Because when love is right, it just is.

Love After Loss: Stepping Back Into Dating

For a long time, I thought that was it for me.

I had experienced a once-in-a-lifetime love. How could I possibly find that again? Did I even want to? And even if I did—how does a woman who hasn't dated since her 20s step back into the world of dating in her 70s?

It felt overwhelming. The world had changed. Dating had changed.

But I had changed, too.

So after years of believing that love wasn't in the cards for me anymore, I made a decision: I would try.

It wasn't easy at first. Dating again after decades was nerve-wracking. I had to relearn everything—from how to meet people to how to recognize what I truly wanted.

But after a few tries, I found my rhythm. I put myself out there. And you know what? I started dating again.

And it turns out—love doesn't have an age limit.

The Biggest Lesson: Be Who You're Looking For

If I've learned one thing from dating again, it's this:

Be who you're looking for.

- If you want someone kind and generous—be kind and generous.
- If you want someone witty and full of laughter— bring laughter into your own life.
- If you want someone who will listen and help you solve problems—be a great listener first.

Because love isn't just about finding the right person. It's about being the right person.

How to Open Yourself to Love Again

1. Believe That Love is Still Meant for You.

If you don't believe love is possible, you'll never truly see it—even when it's standing right in front of you.

2. Let Go of the Timeline.

Love doesn't follow a schedule. You don't have to be in your 20s or 30s to experience deep, soul-filling love. Love happens when it's supposed to happen.

3. Stay Open, Stay Curious.

Be open to meeting new people. You don't have to search for love, but you do have to be available for it.

4. Know That Love Can Look Different Now.

The way you loved at 25 might not be the way you love at 55. And that's okay. Love evolves as we do.

5. Be Yourself.

The best love stories begin when you're living authentically. Don't shrink yourself to fit into someone else's world—let love meet you where you are.

The Truth About Love & Timing

Sometimes, love happens when you least expect it.

I wasn't looking for love when I met my husband. I was headed in an entirely different direction, convinced I already knew what I wanted. But love had other plans.

That's how love works.

It doesn't always come when you want it to. But when it does come? It's exactly when it's supposed to.

So if you're still waiting—keep your heart open.

Because love isn't over for you.

It may be just getting started.

Worrying doesn't take away tomorrow's troubles,

it takes away today's peace.

-Unknown

Secret #9

Start Over *Again*

Starting over.

It's a phrase we hear often, especially after a major life transition—a loss, a career shift, a move, or a change we didn't see coming. But is it really starting over?

I felt as though I was starting over when I transitioned from being a nonprofit executive and community leader to becoming an entrepreneur and running my own business.

But I wasn't.

I had decades of experience, wisdom, leadership, and relationships that didn't disappear just because I made a shift. What I thought was starting over was actually building on everything I had already done.

But there was another transition that felt completely different. One that did make me feel like I had to start over in every sense of the word.

Starting Over After Loss

I lost the three most important people in my life—my husband and my parents—all within a short period of time.

They had been with me my entire life. They had shaped me, supported me, and walked alongside me. And then, suddenly, they were gone.

I didn't know what to do next.

It reminded me of that moment in *Frozen II*, when Anna thinks she's lost everything, and she sings that song— *"The Next Right Thing."*

She doesn't have the answers. She doesn't know how to move forward. She just knows she has to take the next step.

That's exactly how I felt.

I didn't have a plan. I didn't know what life without them looked like. I just had to take the next step.

Starting over after deep loss is different from any other kind of transition. It's not just about making a career move or shifting directions—it's about learning how to live again when the people who shaped your world are no longer in it.

But I learned something along the way.

You're Not Really Starting Over—You're Rebuilding

Starting over doesn't mean going back to zero. You are not a blank slate.

You are a woman with experience, wisdom, resilience, and a story that has shaped you.

You don't have to erase everything that came before to build something new. You simply have to rediscover your purpose and rewrite the story you're telling yourself.

Changing the Narrative: The Story You Tell Yourself Matters

Every time I went through a major transition, I had to rewrite my internal story.

- **When I left my nonprofit career to start my own business, my first thought was: "I'm too old to do this."**

  o I had to change that narrative to: "I am creative, resourceful, and capable of anything I set my mind to."

- **When I lost my parents and husband, I told myself: "I am lost. I have no purpose."**

  o I had to change that to: "I am still here for a reason. I am purposeful, creative, and here to teach and inspire."

Your inner dialogue can either keep you stuck or pull you forward.

If you're starting over, ask yourself: What story am I telling myself? And then ask: Does this story serve me?

How to Rebuild Your Life After a Major Transition

1. Rediscover Your Purpose.

You are here for a reason. Even if it feels like your purpose has changed, it's still there—you just need to uncover it.

2. Get to Know Yourself Again.

Life changes us. Loss changes us. Transitions shift how we see ourselves. Take time to explore who you are today. What do you love? What excites you? What's calling you forward?

3. Change the Narrative.

If you're telling yourself, "It's too late for me"—stop. Rewrite that thought. Replace it with: "I am capable, wise, and prepared for this next chapter."

4. Take Small Steps.

You don't need a full plan right away. Just take the next step. Then another. Then another. Before you know it, you're moving forward.

5. Surround Yourself with Support.

You are not meant to figure this out alone. Seek mentors, friends, or groups that encourage you and remind you who you are.

6.   Allow Yourself to Grieve, But Don't Get Stuck There.

If your transition involves loss, honor it. Feel it. But don't let it define your future.

7.   Rebuild with Intention.

You're not just going through this—you are growing through this. Use this time to build a life that excites you.

8.   You Can Do This Again—And Again

We don't just start over once in life. We start over many times.

Every transition, every shift, every loss, every new beginning—it all requires us to take a deep breath, gather ourselves, and step forward.

But here's the thing:

You've done this before.

And you can do it again.

If it doesn't make you feel fabulous;

don't do it,

don't buy it,

don't wear it,

don't eat it, and

don't keep it.

-Unknown

Secret #10

Leave Behind Your Past

The past is powerful.

Some of it is beautiful—the kind of memories you wrap yourself in like a warm blanket. Some of it is painful—the kind of experiences that leave scars, reminders of what you've been through.

And some of it? Some of it keeps us stuck.

I don't believe in being harsh about letting go of the past, because so much of it is what made us who we are.

I have wonderful childhood memories.

I grew up on the Jersey Shore in a small town where everybody knew everybody. My sister and I used to joke that all the adults in our community must have had secret meetings about us because they knew everything—what kind of grades we were getting, who we were hanging out with, which contests we were supposed to win, and what college we were expected to attend.

It wasn't pressure. It was community. It was care.

That village of people shaped me into the leader I became. It laid the foundation for my career, my drive, and my belief in lifting others up.

But as much as I love those memories, I know this:

You can't move forward if you're always looking in the rearview mirror.

The Past is a Reference, Not a Roadblock

When you're driving a car, you check the rearview mirror—but you don't stare at it.

Because if you did? You'd crash.

The same is true for life. You can't move forward if you're always looking back.

That doesn't mean you ignore your past. You acknowledge it. You learn from it. You cherish the good, you heal from the bad, and then—you drive forward.

Because here's the truth:

The past does not have to define your future.

When Your Past is Still Talking to You

A lot of what holds us back isn't just past experiences— it's the stories we tell ourselves about them.

Sometimes, that's your childhood self talking.

Sometimes, it's the voice of an old teacher, an ex-partner, or a boss who didn't see your worth.

Sometimes, it's the part of you that's afraid to let go.

I get it.

I've been a mother, a wife, a grandmother, a community leader, an entrepreneur, and the first woman in many spaces.

I've had doors opened for me, and I've had them slam in my face.

I've been lifted up, and I've been knocked down hard.

But I refused to let any of it define what came next.

Because every day, I have a choice.

And so do you.

How to Leave the Past Where It Belongs—Behind You

1. Recognize What's Keeping You Stuck.

Is it an old belief? A fear? A story someone told you about yourself that you're still holding onto? Name it. Because once you see it, you can challenge it.

2. Check the Rearview—But Don't Live There.

Look back to learn, to appreciate, to heal. But then? Turn your eyes forward. That's where your life is happening.

3. Rewrite the Narrative.

If your past is telling you, "I'm not good enough"—rewrite it. Replace it with: "I am wise, strong, and prepared for what's next."

4. Embrace Lifelong Learning.

Every single day, your brain has the ability to grow, reshape, and rewire. Neuroplasticity allows you to keep learning, keep evolving, and keep becoming whoever you want to be.

5. Forgive—Yourself and Others.

Not for them. For you. Carrying resentment weighs you down. Let it go so you can walk freely into your future.

6. Decide That Today is More Important Than Yesterday.

The past already happened. But today? Today is still yours to shape.

Your Future is Waiting

I'm not saying forget your past. I'm saying don't let it steal your future.

Take the lessons. Keep the love. Release the weight.

Because your next chapter isn't behind you—it's ahead.

And it's going to be amazing.

Be fearless in the pursuit of

what sets your soul on fire.

-Unknown

Secret #11

Use Your Glowing Personality

There's something magnetic about a person who radiates energy, warmth, and confidence.

I don't mean the kind of energy that comes from caffeine or a good night's sleep—though those help. I'm talking about a deeper energy. The kind that comes from gratitude, from self-awareness, from knowing exactly who you are and showing up fully in the world.

Some people call it charisma. Some call it presence.

I call it owning your glow.

Energy is Everything

I've hired hundreds of people in my career. And let me tell you, first impressions matter.

Science says we size someone up within seconds of meeting them, but even before science confirmed it, I already knew it to be true. It's not just about how you look—it's about the energy you bring into a room.

You can feel it. We all can.

There are people who walk in, and suddenly the air shifts. They bring light, confidence, and warmth. They make people feel seen. They make people feel good.

And then, there are the life-force drainers.

You know the ones—the people who, when they walk into a space, suck the energy right out of it. They bring negativity, complaints, doubt, or just a general dullness that makes you feel exhausted even after a short interaction.

Which one do you want to be?

Because here's the truth: Anyone can have charisma.

It's not something you're born with. It's something you cultivate.

How to Glow From the Inside Out

1. Turn Wisdom into Energy.

They say youth is full of energy, and aging is about slowing down. I don't believe that. When you own your wisdom and experience, it doesn't drain you—it fuels you. Age isn't a decline—it's a buildup of everything you've learned, everything you've become. Let that empower you.

2. Be the Light in the Room.

My parents raised me to greet people with warmth— always. Growing up in a small town, it was expected that when you saw someone, you'd speak—whether you knew them or not. "Good morning!" "How are you today?"

There's an energy in that simple act. A smile, a kind word, an open posture—it changes how people see you. More importantly, it changes how you see yourself.

3. Protect Your Energy.

Not everyone deserves access to your energy. If someone consistently drains you, set boundaries. Walk away when you need to. Protect your glow at all costs.

4. Live With Gratitude.

Gratitude isn't just about being thankful—it's about seeing life as abundant. When you walk through life with gratitude, you naturally exude confidence, joy, and a presence that draws people in. People don't remember what you wore. They remember how you made them feel.

5. Smile With Your Whole Being.

Ever met someone whose smile reaches their eyes? It's contagious. It changes the energy in a space. A true, warm, open smile isn't just about looking friendly—it's about feeling fully alive.

6. Show Up With Intention.

Whether you're walking into a boardroom, a coffee shop, or your own living room, bring your best self. Carry yourself with presence. Stand tall. Speak with confidence. Make eye contact. Own your space.

7. Refuse to Be Invisible.

There's a myth that after a certain age, women start to fade into the background. Society tries to make us believe we should shrink, soften, step aside.

No.

You are more vibrant, relevant, and impactful than ever. Walk like you believe it.

Your Glow is Your Power

Your energy—your presence—is what makes people remember you. It's what makes people want to be around you, listen to you, work with you, love you.

And the best part?

It has nothing to do with age.

It has everything to do with how you show up in the world.

So stand tall.

Smile big.

Radiate confidence.

And never dim your light.

Because the world needs it.

It's not who you are that holds you back.

It's who you think you're not.

-Unknown

Secret #12

Pay Attention To These Stress Signs

Stress isn't just an inconvenience. It's a killer.

For years, I thought I was handling it. I had built a life full of responsibilities—an important career, a family I adored, a deep commitment to my community. I was doing it all.

Then one morning, I walked into my office early—before most people arrived, as usual. I sat at my desk. And I couldn't move.

I wasn't paralyzed. But my body simply refused to go through the motions. It was as if every demand, every expectation, every obligation had piled up so high that my body finally said, "Enough."

I knew something had to change.

The Ice Water Moment That Changed Everything

I talked to my mother about it. I told her everything—the job, the long hours, the family responsibilities, the community work, the constant pressure to keep pushing forward.

She listened. And then she said something that hit me like a cold slap of ice water to my face:

"I'm sorry for what you're doing to yourself."

Not, "I'm sorry for how much you have to deal with."

Not, "I'm sorry life is so hard right now."

But "I'm sorry for what YOU are putting yourself through."

That's when it hit me: Stress wasn't just something happening to me. It was something I was allowing.

It wasn't just the demands of my job or my family—it was how I was handling it.

And that moment set me on a path.

I didn't become an expert at eliminating stress overnight. But I started working on it. And over time, I realized something:

Stress isn't something we should manage. It's something we should eliminate.

Because stress—unchecked, unchallenged, and unaddressed—kills.

SEO: The Silent Killer

I came up with my own term for what I had been experiencing: SEO.

No, not search engine optimization.

SEO: Stress. Exhaustion. Overwhelm.

It's what too many women go through every single day.

We wear it like a badge of honor—multitasking, handling everything, pushing through the exhaustion. But at what cost?

If you're constantly in a cycle of **SEO—Stress, Exhaustion, and Overwhelm—**your body is sending you a warning. And it's time to listen.

Warning Signs Your Stress is Out of Control

1. You wake up tired—even after a full night's sleep.

If your body never truly rests, no amount of sleep will feel like enough.

2. You feel like you're always rushing, but never catching up.

No matter how much you do, the to-do list never gets shorter.

3. You snap at people you love for no reason.

You're not angry at them—you're just depleted.

4. Your body is holding onto tension.

Tight shoulders, headaches, digestion issues? Stress manifests physically.

5. You don't remember the last time you truly felt joy.

If happiness feels distant, it's a sign you've been running on empty for too long.

How to Start Eliminating Stress (Not Just Managing It)

1. Redefine What's Essential.

Not everything is urgent. Not everything is your responsibility. Say no more often.

2. Listen to Your Body.

Your body sends signals before it shuts down. Don't wait for a breaking point.

3. Give Yourself Permission to Rest.

Rest is not laziness. Rest is survival.

4. Create Space for What Refuels You.

Whether it's quiet time, movement, or deep conversations—prioritize what brings you back to life.

5. Challenge the Narrative That You Have to Do It All.

The world will not fall apart if you take care of yourself. But you might, if you don't.

6.   Live in Your Purpose—Unapologetically.

When you are fully aligned with what you are meant to do—without compromise, without waffling, without fear—stress loses its grip. Purpose fuels energy, passion, and resilience.

7.   Eliminate People Who Drain Your Energy.

Some people bring light, and some people suck the life out of you. Protect your space.

8.   Decide That Today is More Important Than Yesterday.

The past already happened. But today? Today is still yours to shape.

Your Health is Non-Negotiable

I know how it feels to push through, to carry it all, to convince yourself you can handle just a little bit more.

But at what cost?

You don't have to prove your strength by burning yourself out.

You don't have to wait until you're too exhausted to function before you make a change.

Take control of your SEO.

Because the best version of you—the happiest, healthiest, most vibrant version of you—doesn't live in stress, exhaustion, and overwhelm.

She lives in balance.

She lives in peace.

She lives in joy.

And she's waiting for you to choose her.

The vibrant life begins at the end of your comfort zone.

- Unknown

Secret #13

Dress Your Finest

—⊗—

Fashion is more than just clothes.

It's self-expression. It's confidence. It's reinvention.

I've used fashion as a tool to mark new beginnings, major transitions, and high-visibility moments in my life. Every time I stepped into a new career move, a leadership role, or a fresh chapter, I used it as an opportunity to reimagine my look—to reinvent myself.

It might have been a new hairstyle. A signature accessory. A completely different approach to dressing.

One year, I became obsessed with pearls.

I didn't just wear a pearl necklace—I built a whole collection. Rings, bracelets, earrings, layered strands of pearls. Every time you saw me, I had pearls on.

Then, after a few years, my perspective shifted again, and I tried something new.

And I still do this today.

Because reinvention is power.

Midlife is the Best Time to Create Your Signature Style

There is something deliciously freeing about midlife.

You can wear what you want. You can change your style whenever you feel like it. You can set trends instead of following them.

This is the time when we get to define what looking our best means to us.

It's not about dressing "age-appropriately."

It's not about following anyone else's rules.

It's about feeling your finest, on your terms.

The Power of Signature Style

I believe in statement pieces.

Those little details that people see and immediately associate with you.

- Maybe you always wear a scarf—a bold pop of color or an elegant silk wrap.

- Maybe you love hats—classic fedoras, chic berets, or wide-brimmed sun hats.

- Maybe it's a certain color palette that makes you feel powerful.

- Or maybe you, like me, rotate your style every few years to reflect who you are becoming.

It's a form of personal branding. It's a way of saying, "This is me."

Your Finest Style is Yours to Define

1. Experiment & Evolve.

Every few years, I take a fresh look at my wardrobe. What feels like me now? What needs to change? Reinventing your look can be as small as a new lipstick color or as bold as a whole new wardrobe.

2. Shop Your Own Closet.

You probably have beautiful pieces you haven't worn in years. I'll pull out brooches from my 30s and 40s, pin them on, and suddenly people stop me and ask, "Where did you get that?" Fashion doesn't expire—it comes back around.

3. Own What You Love.

If you love pearls—wear pearls. If you love oversized earrings, wear them boldly. This is your time to wear what makes you feel good.

4. Dress for Joy.

If an outfit makes you happy, it's the right outfit.

5. Be the Trendsetter.

Midlife is not about fading into the background. It's about showing up, standing out, and leading the way.

You Define What Looking Your Best Means

Dressing your finest isn't about impressing others.

It's about feeling powerful in your own skin.

And at this stage in life? You make the rules.

So wear the hat. Pull out the vintage brooch. Reinvent your look—again and again.

Because your finest style is the one that makes you feel unstoppable.

I'm gonna make the rest of my life, the best of my life.

-Unknown

Secret #14

What You Should Wear On A Date

Dating again after years—or even decades—can feel like stepping into a whole new world.

When I started dating again, I realized how much had changed since my 20s. But one thing remained the same: the way you present yourself matters.

That doesn't mean dressing for someone else. It means dressing in a way that makes you feel confident, comfortable, and ready to enjoy yourself.

And yes, there's a difference between comfort and being comfortable.

Confidence Starts with Feeling Good in What You Wear

Let's get the basics out of the way:

- Smell good—but don't overdo the perfume. A light, fresh scent is lovely, but too much fragrance can be overwhelming.

- Good hygiene is non-negotiable. Clean hair, well-manicured nails, and fresh breath—the little things matter.

- Take time with your appearance. Whether it's a casual date or a dressy one, put in the effort. It shows.

Dress for the Setting, Not Just the Date

Where you're going should influence what you wear.

I remember one of my first dates—I think it was the second one—we went to the movies. Now, I know myself. I love popcorn, and I also know I will end up spilling it. So for that date, I made sure to wear something stylish but also practical—something that wouldn't suffer from a few stray popcorn kernels.

That was completely different from my first date, where I put extra thought into a polished, elegant look because we were going to a nice dinner.

So, before you pick out your outfit, think about where you're going.

- Dinner Date? Something polished but not overly formal. A stylish dress, chic blouse with tailored pants, or an elegant jumpsuit can be great options.

- Movie Date? Casual but put-together—jeans with a stylish top, a casual dress, or something easy to move in.

- Museum or Cultural Event? Something artistic and expressive—this is a great time to wear bold accessories or a statement piece.

- Outdoor Date? Dress appropriately for the weather, but make sure you still feel stylish. Comfortable does not mean sloppy.

At this stage in life, we've been to plenty of these places before—we know what works.

Comfort vs. Being Comfortable

Comfort doesn't mean baggy clothes, shapeless outfits, or flat shoes (unless that's your preference).

I'm comfortable in heels—so if I feel my best in them, I'll wear them. But if you're someone who hates heels, then don't force it.

The key is to wear something that makes you feel good. Because when you feel good, you exude confidence.

A Few Fun Tricks to Try

1. Flatter Your Figure.

I don't believe in wearing overly revealing clothes on a first date, but I do believe in dressing in a way that highlights your best features. Find silhouettes that make you feel amazing.

2. Play with Color.

I read once that asking your date what their favorite colors are and then wearing those colors creates an instant connection. I tried it. It works. It's a fun way to add a little extra touch to your look.

3. Accessorize with Personality.

Whether it's a signature necklace, a bold pair of earrings, or a statement scarf—accessories add personality to your outfit.

4. Dress to Have Fun.

Dating should be enjoyable! Let your outfit reflect that. If you feel good in what you're wearing, you'll be more relaxed, and your personality will shine.

Most Important Rule? Be You.

Dressing for a date isn't about impressing someone else.

It's about showing up as your best self.

So whether you wear heels or flats, bold colors or neutrals, a statement dress or jeans and a top—make sure it's an outfit that makes you feel powerful, comfortable, and most of all, YOU.

Because the best thing you can wear on any date?

Confidence.

Beauty isn't about having a pretty face. It's about having a pretty mind, pretty heart, and pretty soul.

-Unknown

Secret #15

Over 50? What's Next In Life

Fifty years.

Half a century of life, experiences, lessons, and transformation.

Turning 50—or stepping into any phase of midlife—isn't just another birthday. It's a moment when many of us stop and ask:

What's next?

And it makes sense.

Midlife is a time of change.

- Our bodies change.
- Our responsibilities shift.
- We experience loss—whether it's parents, loved ones, or even parts of our identity that no longer fit.
- We ask deeper questions about purpose, legacy, and what truly matters.
- We may go through career transitions, an empty nest, or simply feel the need for something more.

Some call it a midlife crisis. I call it a midlife awakening.

Because this is your moment—to take all the wisdom, all the experience, all the lessons of your first 50 years and decide how you're going to use them to create the next, most powerful chapter of your life.

But here's the thing:

Reinvention doesn't happen by accident. It happens by design.

And that's why I created The NEXT Steps Framework.

From Transforming Communities to Transforming Lives

My entire career has been about transformation.

In my nonprofit work, I helped individuals, organizations, and communities move from where they were to where they wanted to be. I worked with schools, neighborhoods, and social issues—raising over $100 million to help people create change.

When I stepped into entrepreneurship, that transformation focus didn't change.

I just started working with leaders, executives, and entrepreneurs—helping them navigate their own transformations.

I've combined my academic training (a doctorate, a master's, and years of study in leadership and transformation) with real-world, hands-on experience to create a simple, clear framework for anyone asking:

What's next for me?

The NEXT Steps Framework: A Roadmap for Your Next Chapter

Transformation isn't about guessing. It's about having a process.

The NEXT Steps Framework is designed to help you go from where you are now to where you truly want to be.

1: Change the Narrative

- We've talked about this before, but it's worth repeating: the story you tell yourself shapes your future.

- Are you telling yourself, *"I'm too old for this"?* Or are you saying, *"I am creative, resourceful, and capable of anything"*?

- Rewrite your internal dialogue so that it supports where you want to go.

2: Create a Vibrant Vision

- This isn't about settling—it's about limitless possibility.

- If you could do anything, be anywhere, create whatever you want—what would that look like?

- Midlife is your chance to design your next chapter with intention.

3: Build the Plan

- Vision without a plan is just a dream.

- This is where you get strategic—what steps will move you closer to the life you want?

- A game plan isn't about control. It's about direction.

4: Find and Give Joy

- The older we get, the more we realize what truly matters.

- This step is about prioritizing what brings you joy, fulfillment, and meaning.

- Because at the end of the day, success without joy isn't success at all.

Midlife Isn't an Ending—It's a Beginning

For years, I helped transform communities.

Now, I help people transform themselves.

And if you're reading this, I want you to know something:

Your next chapter can be whatever you want it to be.

You are not stuck. You are not too old. You are not out of options.

You are at the perfect moment to design a life that excites you.

So take a breath.

And then take your NEXT step.

Because your best years?

They're still ahead.

It all begins and ends in your mind.

What you give power to, has power over you, if you allow it.

-Unknown

Secret #16

Pause Daily

People talk a lot about work-life balance—but is there really such a thing?

I know so many high-achieving women—myself included—who have spent years chasing that elusive balance.

We build careers, raise families, take care of our communities, support others, and keep everything moving forward. And yet, we rarely stop to take care of ourselves.

I once had an incredible conversation with an expert in rest and work-life integration, and she said something that stopped me in my tracks:

"High-achieving women don't struggle with work. They struggle with rest."

And I knew exactly what she meant.

Because we've been conditioned to believe that doing more makes us valuable. That pausing is a weakness. That if we're not being productive, we're falling behind.

But the truth is, if you don't pause, reset, and refuel, you won't be able to sustain the very success you've worked so hard to achieve.

The Pause: A Simple but Powerful Tool

There is so much power in simply stopping.

Not quitting. Not giving up. Just pausing.

Taking 10 minutes to breathe.

Taking a step back before reacting.

Taking time to rest—before burnout forces you to.

Pausing isn't about wasting time. It's about reclaiming your energy, your clarity, and your peace.

What Happens When We Never Pause?

1. You Burn Out Faster.

If you're always running at full speed, your body and mind will eventually force you to stop—whether you like it or not.

2. You Lose Sight of What's Important.

When you're always busy, you don't have time to reflect on whether the things you're working so hard for actually matter.

3. You Miss the Joy in the Moment.

If you're always thinking about the next task, the next goal, the next responsibility—you never get to fully experience what's happening right now.

Different Types of Rest: More Than Just Sleep

Most people think of rest as just getting more sleep. But there are many different types of rest—some of which you may be deeply deprived of without even realizing it.

- Maybe you're mentally exhausted from constantly problem-solving.

- Maybe you're emotionally drained from holding everything together for others.

- Maybe you need creative rest—a chance to be inspired again.

True rest isn't just about stopping. It's about restoring what has been depleted.

How to Use the Pause to Break the Cycle

1. Build Pauses Into Your Day.

Take five minutes between meetings to breathe. Pause before reacting to an email. Give yourself space before making big decisions.

2. Learn to Say No Without Guilt.

Every time you say "yes" to something that drains you, you're saying "no" to something that could restore you.

3. Identify Your Rest Deficits.

Are you physically tired? Mentally drained? Emotionally exhausted? Figure out where you're depleted and be intentional about replenishing.

4. Stop Chasing Balance—Create Alignment.

Instead of trying to juggle everything perfectly, focus on aligning your time and energy with what truly matters to you.

5. Give Yourself Permission to Stop.

Rest isn't a luxury—it's a requirement. You don't need to earn rest. You need to prioritize it.

Rest Isn't Weakness—It's Strength

For years, I convinced myself that I could just push through. That I could keep going no matter how exhausted I felt.

Now, I know better.

I know that pausing isn't a sign of failure—it's a strategy for success.

So take a breath. Step back. Pause.

Because the stronger, wiser, more powerful version of you?

She's waiting on the other side of rest.

I always wonder why birds stay in the same place

when they can fly anywhere on the earth.

Then, I ask myself the same question.

-Unknown

Secret #17

Creating Fearless Opportunities

Fear is a powerful thing.

It can push you forward or hold you back. It can fuel change or keep you stuck.

And for so many people over 50, fear shows up as hesitation—wondering if it's too late, if the best years are behind them, if they should even bother trying something new.

I've had those moments too.

When I left my long-standing career in nonprofit leadership to become an entrepreneur, I was afraid.

- *What if I failed?*
- *What if no one took me seriously at this stage in my life?*
- *What if everything I had built before was all I'd ever achieve?*

But here's what I learned:

Fear isn't a stop sign—it's a decision point.

You can let it hold you back.

Or you can use it as fuel to move forward.

What Fear Really Is

Fear is rarely about the thing itself.

- It's not about changing careers.
- It's not about starting a new relationship.
- It's not about stepping into something unfamiliar.

It's about the stories we tell ourselves.

The myths, the limiting beliefs, the doubts that whisper in our ears and make us second-guess ourselves.

And those stories? They aren't real.

They're based on outdated narratives, past disappointments, and societal expectations that say, *"Stay in your lane. Play it safe. You've missed your chance."*

But let me tell you something:

You are never too old to create new opportunities for yourself.

The Biggest Myths That Hold People Back

1. "I'm too old to start something new."

   o No, you're not.

- o Some of the most successful entrepreneurs, leaders, and creators hit their stride after 50.

- o Your experience, wisdom, and resilience make you more prepared—not less.

2. "I've already invested too much in my current path."

- o Your past isn't a waste—it's a foundation.

- o Everything you've done has prepared you for what's next.

3. "It's too risky to make a change now."

- o Staying stuck is the real risk.

- o You don't have to take a leap—just take the first step.

How to Create Fearless Opportunities

1. Challenge the Stories in Your Head.

- o Every time fear tells you, *"I can't,"* respond with *"Why not?"*

- o Start questioning the limits you've placed on yourself.

2. Reframe Fear as Excitement.

- o Fear and excitement feel almost identical in the body.

- o Instead of saying *"I'm scared,"* try saying *"I'm excited for what's next."*

3. Take One Bold Step at a Time.

- o Fear grows in hesitation.
- o The more you act in spite of fear, the more confident you become.

4. Surround Yourself with Possibility Thinkers.

- o If you're constantly around people who play small, you'll start doing the same.
- o Seek out people who challenge you to think bigger.

5. Give Yourself Permission to Start Over.

- o Reinvention is not a sign of failure. It's a sign of courage.

Fear Might Always Be There—But It Doesn't Have to Lead

Courage isn't the absence of fear.

It's deciding that your dreams, your future, and your next chapter matter more than your doubts.

So the question isn't, "What *if I fail?*"

The real question is, "What if I don't try?"

Because on the other side of fear?

That's where your greatest opportunities are waiting.

Don't cry over the past, it's gone.

Don't stress about the future, it hasn't arrived.

Live in the present and make it beautiful.

\- Unknown

Secret # 18

Vibrant Women Leaving A Legacy

---❖---

At a certain point in life, you start thinking about more than just what you've accomplished—you start thinking about what you're leaving behind.

Legacy isn't just about money or material wealth.

It's about impact. Influence. The lessons and values you pass down.

It's about how you've shaped the world around you—your family, your community, your work, and the generations coming behind you.

And for vibrant women over 50, this is the time to be intentional about it.

What Does It Mean to Leave a Legacy?

For me, legacy has always been tied to leadership and transformation.

I think about my father, a transformational leader who dedicated his life to changing communities, creating opportunities, and mentoring others. He wanted to leave behind more than just memories—he wanted to leave instructions.

Lessons on how to lead, build, and uplift.

And then there's my mother.

She left a legacy in a different way.

She was a teacher, a poet, and a woman who deeply impacted the lives of others. Even today, when I go back to my small hometown, people still talk about Miss Jones.

They tell me how she was the best teacher they ever had. How she believed in them, pushed them, and made them feel like they could do anything.

She hasn't been in a classroom for years. She's gone on to her glory. But her impact is still alive.

That's pure legacy.

It's a reminder that legacy isn't about what you do for yourself—it's about what you do for others.

Why Legacy Matters More Than Ever After 50

This stage of life brings clarity.

- You know what truly matters.
- You know what's worth your time—and what isn't.

- You start thinking about the mark you want to leave on the world.

Leaving a legacy isn't about being remembered.

It's about making an impact that lasts beyond you.

How to Create a Lasting Legacy

1. Mentor the next generation.

   o Share what you know. Guide those coming behind you.

   o Whether it's in your career, your family, or your community—be a mentor.

2. Document your wisdom.

   o Write it down. Speak it. Teach it.

   o My mother wrote poetry—her words still live on today. Your story, your lessons, your journey—they matter.

3. Create opportunities for others.

   o Whether through leadership, philanthropy, or simply supporting the people around you—use your influence to open doors.

4. Live your values.

   o Legacy isn't just about what you say—it's about how you live.

   o Be the example of what's possible.

5. Give back through volunteering.

- One of the most powerful ways to leave a legacy is by giving your time.

- Volunteering allows you to make a direct impact in areas that matter to you. Whether it's mentoring young professionals, helping a local nonprofit, or supporting a cause, your time and skills can change lives.

6. Build a philanthropic legacy.

- Giving back isn't just about time—it's also about financial generosity.

- Whether it's supporting organizations that align with your values, establishing scholarships, or making charitable donations, financial giving ensures your impact continues beyond your lifetime.

7. Think beyond today.

- The choices you make now shape the future.

- Ask yourself: *What am I building that will last?*

Your Legacy is Happening Now

A legacy isn't something you leave behind when you're gone.

You're creating it right now.

Every life you touch, every lesson you share, every way you show up—that's your legacy in motion.

So if you're over 50, vibrant, and full of life—don't just think about legacy. Live it.

Because the impact you make today?

That's what lasts forever.

The past is a place of reference,

not a place of residence.

-Unknown

Secret #19

Add More Color to Your Life

Color is energy.

It awakens the senses, shifts your mood, and brings life into the spaces around you.

I've always loved black—there's nothing sharper than a sleek black dress. Black is powerful, classic, and timeless. And when you add a pop of bold color—through accessories, shoes, or even a bright red lip—it's even more striking.

But there was a time when my world felt too dark.

The Moment I Realized I Needed More Color

After experiencing deep loss, I started feeling like everything around me reflected that heaviness.

One day, I looked at my wardrobe, my home, and my surroundings—and I noticed so much black, so much gray, so much neutral.

It wasn't that I had intentionally chosen those colors as a statement. It was more that they had crept in, slowly, silently, matching how I felt inside.

That's when I made a decision:

I was going to bring color back into my life.

- I added vibrant pieces to my wardrobe.

- I brought bold accessories into my outfits.

- I added rich, lively colors to my home—throw pillows, curtains, and artwork that made me feel alive.

And something changed.

Color Isn't Just About Style—It's About Energy

Adding color isn't just about fashion or home décor—it's about vibrancy, energy, and self-expression.

It's about how certain colors can lift your mood, ignite creativity, and bring joy.

Think about it:

- Red brings power, passion, and strength.

- Yellow radiates warmth, optimism, and energy.

- Green feels calming, fresh, and full of life.

- Blue inspires confidence, peace, and clarity.

- Purple signals wisdom, creativity, and individuality.

Even a small pop of color—a statement necklace, a pair of bold shoes, or a striking piece of art—can transform how you feel.

Bringing More Color Into Your Life

1. Start with What You Wear.

   o If you love black, keep it! But try adding a bold handbag, colorful scarf, or striking jewelry.

2. Refresh Your Home with Color.

   o You don't have to repaint your walls—a few colorful pillows, curtains, or flowers can completely change the energy of a room.

3. Experiment with Different Shades.

   o If you're not used to wearing color, try deep jewel tones or rich earthy hues to start.

4. Let Color Reflect Your Mood.

   o Some days, you may feel powerful in red. Other days, you may want the calm of soft blues or the creativity of purples. Let color be part of your self-expression.

5. Surround Yourself with Vibrant Energy.

- Color isn't just about what you wear or what's in your home—it's about who and what surrounds you.

- Seek out people, experiences, and environments that bring brightness into your life.

Life is Meant to Be Lived in Full Color

I realized that color wasn't just something I added to my wardrobe or my home—it was something I brought back into my life.

More laughter. More adventure. More boldness.

Because life isn't meant to be lived in shades of gray.

It's meant to be vibrant, expressive, and full of color.

So take a look around—where can you add more color?

Because the brighter you allow yourself to shine, the more alive you'll feel.

You must learn a new way to think

before you can master a new way to be.

- Marianne Williamson

Secret #20

Love & Vibrant Living

❖

Love at first sight is one thing. Staying together for decades is another.

When I met Otha Williams, I knew almost instantly that we would be together. By the end of that same week, we were shopping for furniture. Ten months later, we were married.

And we stayed together for 40 years.

But here's the thing about marriage—even when you start with a love that feels undeniable, there are moments when you stop and ask yourself big questions.

And for many, that moment comes in midlife.

The Midlife Marriage Question: Do We Still Belong Together?

Something happens when you reach 50.

You look at your life differently. You reflect on where you've been, what you've built, and where you want to go. And if you've been in a long-term relationship, you might find yourself looking at your partner and wondering:

- *Do I still want to spend the rest of my life with this person?*

- *Are we growing together or growing apart?*

- *Who am I now, and does this relationship still fit?*

It's a normal question.

Life changes. Bodies change. Responsibilities shift. Kids leave home. Careers slow down or speed up.

And the marriage that worked in your 30s and 40s may not feel the same in your 50s and beyond.

That doesn't mean the love is gone.

It means the relationship has to evolve.

The Foundation of a Strong Marriage

If cancer hadn't taken Otha, we'd still be together. I know that. Because we made it through the rough patches, the questioning seasons, and the moments when staying felt harder than leaving.

We made it because we had a foundation.

Some things in a relationship can shift and change—but some things must be solid from the start. Otha and I shared core values, and I believe that's one of the biggest reasons we lasted.

We both believed deeply in:

- Family. No matter what, family came first. We gave everything we could to our children.

- Community. We were committed to uplifting the people around us and making an impact beyond just our home.

- Authenticity. We didn't play games, and we didn't pretend to be something we weren't.

- Financial Alignment. We agreed on how money should be managed and made sure we were always on the same page.

- Intimacy & Communication. We constantly talked about what intimacy meant at different phases of our lives. Because it changes—and you have to be willing to talk about it.

When a couple doesn't share the same core values, the relationship becomes harder to sustain. Love is important, but alignment in key areas makes love last.

What Kept Us Together for 40 Years

1. We Grew Together, Not Apart.
   o People change. The key is to support each other's growth instead of resisting it.

2. We Kept Talking—Even When It Was Hard.
   o Silence kills relationships. You have to talk, even about the uncomfortable stuff.

3. We Didn't Stop Dating Each Other.
   o Years together don't replace quality time.

o   Go on dates. Laugh together. Have fun.

4. We Respected Each Other More Than We Wanted to Be Right.

o   Winning an argument isn't worth losing the relationship. Respect comes first.

5. We Redefined Intimacy Over the Years.

o   Intimacy isn't just physical—it's closeness, connection, and understanding.

o   We talked about what we needed at different phases of our lives.

6. We Talked About Money—A Lot.

o   Financial stress can break a marriage.

o   We stayed on the same page about spending, saving, and planning.

7. We Chose Each Other—Again and Again.

o   Love isn't just a feeling. It's a decision you make every single day.

Love Changes, But It Doesn't Have to Fade

Long-term love isn't about keeping things the same. It's about growing through the changes together.

At 50, 60, 70, and beyond, your relationship won't look like it did when you first started.

But that doesn't mean it can't be stronger, deeper, and more fulfilling than ever.

The key?

Keep choosing each other.

Every single day.

What's Next for You?

The Secret to Turning Inspiration into Action

You've read the secrets, reflected on the possibilities, and maybe even started picturing what your next chapter could look like.

You know that life over 50 isn't about slowing down—it's about stepping into your next season with purpose, confidence, and vibrancy.

But here's what I've seen over and over again.

Too many of us get stuck between inspiration and action. We know they want more, but we're not sure how to move forward. You feel the pull for something new—a career shift, a fresh purpose, a more fulfilling life—but don't have a clear path to get there. And without a plan, it's easy to stay in place, waiting, wondering if now is the right time.

Therefore, I created The NEXT Steps Framework.

This isn't just a concept—it's a proven strategy that I've developed through years of coaching midlife men and women through reinvention. It's based on what works.

What I've seen transform lives. What I've lived through myself. Because I know what it feels like to stand at a crossroads, uncertain of the next step.

And I also know that with the right approach, you can move from stuck to unstoppable.

The NEXT Steps Framework: A Simple Guide to Moving Forward with Confidence

◆ Change the Narrative – Identify and challenge the limiting beliefs that have kept you from taking action. You're not too old, it's not too late, and yes, you absolutely can.

◆ Create a Vibrant Vision – Get clear on what you really want. What does your ideal next chapter look like? What excites you? What's calling you forward?

◆ Build the Plan – Map out your steps with intention. Define what needs to happen, when, and how.

◆ Find and Give Joy – Because success isn't just about what you achieve. It's about fulfillment, connection, and creating a legacy that matters.

This framework is not about starting over—it's about starting intentionally.

Your Next Chapter Starts Now. Let's Map It Out Together.

I don't believe in "one-size-fits-all" advice.

You deserve a plan that's tailored to you—your goals, your values, your next chapter. That's why I'd love to connect with you personally.

Visit

www.drgenevaspeaks.com or https://bit.ly/3ruTJTH to book a complimentary strategy call.

101 Things To Do When You Turn 50

Feeling stuck, uncertain, or wondering what's next?

You're not alone.

Midlife isn't about slowing down—it's your time to treasure life, do what you love relentlessly, and move ahead on your own terms.

But if you're wondering, What should I do now? or How can I make the most of this stage?—this guide is for you.

Inside *101 Things To Do When You Turn 50,* you'll find:

✓☐ The real scoop on what's happening in the lives of women over 50 (so you know you're not alone)

✓☐ Smart ways to stay ahead of the game and make midlife your best season yet

✓☐ Money wisdom—decisions that set you up for success

✓☐ Bucket list inspiration—where to travel without breaking the bank

✓☐ Retirement insider tips (because planning now makes all the difference)

✓☐ Bold, fun, and surprising ideas to create a life you love

If you're feeling stuck or unsure about what's next, this guide will give you fresh ideas, clear steps, and the inspiration to take action.

⬇ Download your FREE copy now →

https://stan.store/drgenevaspeaks/p/get-101-things-to-do-when-you-turn-50-